中英双语版

企鹅经典 名人大发现

迈克尔·杰克逊

[美] 梅根·斯泰恩（Megan Stine）◎著 [美] 约瑟夫·J.M. 基（Joseph J. M. Qiu）◎绘 叶雯熙◎译

Who Was Michael Jackson?

湖南科学技术出版社 小博集 BOOKY KIDS

·长沙·

著作权合同登记号：字18-2024-201

图书在版编目（CIP）数据

名人大发现. 迈克尔 · 杰克逊 ：汉英对照 /（美）梅根 · 斯泰恩（Megan Stine）著 ；叶雯熙译 ；（美）约瑟夫 · J.M.基（Joseph J. M. Qiu）绘. -- 长沙 ：湖南科学技术出版社，2025. 1. --（企鹅经典）. -- ISBN 978-7-5710-3272-2

Ⅰ. H319. 4

中国国家版本馆CIP数据核字第202433LP05号

上架建议：科普读物

QI' E JINGDIAN · MINGREN DA FAXIAN：ZHONG-YING SHUANGYU BAN MAIKEER JIEKEXUN

企鹅经典 · 名人大发现：中英双语版　迈克尔 · 杰克逊

著　　者：[美] 梅根 · 斯泰恩（Megan Stine）
绘　　者：[美] 约瑟夫 · J.M.基（Joseph J. M. Qiu）
译　　者：叶雯熙
出 版 人：潘晓山
责任编辑：刘　竞
策划出品：李　炜　张苗苗　文赛峰
策划编辑：马　瑄
特约编辑：杜佳美
营销编辑：付　佳　杨　朔　周晓茜
装帧设计：利　锐
内文排版：金锋工作室
出　　版：湖南科学技术出版社
　　　　　（湖南省长沙市芙蓉中路416号　邮编：410008）
网　　址：www.hnstp.com
印　　刷：三河市航远印刷有限公司
经　　销：新华书店
开　　本：875 mm × 1230 mm 1/32
字　　数：103千字
印　　张：5.125
版　　次：2025年1月第1版
印　　次：2025年1月第1次印刷
书　　号：ISBN 978-7-5710-3272-2
定　　价：22.00元

若有质量问题，请致电质量监督电话：010-59096394　　团购电话：010-59320018

目　录

Contents

谁是迈克尔·杰克逊？

加利福尼亚州，帕萨迪纳市。

在 1983 年的一场演唱会上，迈克尔·杰克逊缓缓走到舞台边缘。他买了一顶和他最新音乐视频里同款的间谍帽。关于如何在接下来的这首歌中用好这顶帽子，迈克尔已经有了主意——他真心希望这个主意能够奏效。

这场在帕萨迪纳市政礼堂举办的演唱会将在电视上播出，届时将有五千万人收看。有很多著名歌手已经在此登台演出，现在是迈克尔大放异彩的时候了。

迈克尔·杰克逊已经是全球最著名的流行歌星了，但他从不满足。他想要呈现让人终生难忘的舞台表演。他想让观众为之疯狂！

随着音乐响起，迈克尔戴上帽子开始舞动。观众们立刻起身沸腾起来。他们尖叫着、欢呼着。他们认出了这顶帽子，知道这首歌是《比利·琼》。

迈克尔身着一件闪闪发亮的黑色夹克、一件银色衬衫和一只白色手套，他的舞步前无古人，后无来者！昨晚他在厨房练习了这些舞蹈动作，抖腿、顶胯、用脚击打地面。他把帽子扔离舞台，动作行云流水，台下的观众又一次陷入疯狂。

随后，在歌曲进行时，他做了一件令人惊奇的事情。他向后滑去，但看上去像是在往前走。他把这个称为月球漫步！月球漫步虽仅仅持续了五秒，但它已经足够令人称奇。

在这首歌的结尾，每个人都站起来了。人群欢呼着。他走下舞台后，全家人给他献上了吻。没有人会忘记月球漫步。事实上，这是迈克尔·杰克逊最著名的舞步。

但是迈克尔开心吗？并不。人们爱这场表演，他很高兴，但他认为他还能表演得更好。月球漫步结束后的那个大旋转，他没有用脚尖立住足够长的时间。

对迈克尔·杰克逊来说，没有最好，只有更好。他

一直想做个完美的人，所以他努力工作，来实现他的梦想——成为史上作品最畅销的歌手。这个原因促使他成为流行音乐之王。

第一章

小房子，大梦想

迈克尔·约瑟夫·杰克逊在 1958 年 8 月 29 日出生于印第安纳州的加里。杰克逊一家的房子很小，拥挤不堪。迈克尔有四个哥哥和两个姐姐。莫琳，也被称为瑞比，是年龄最大的。然后是杰基、蒂托、杰曼、拉托亚和马龙。迈克尔出生几年后，兰迪出生。珍妮特·杰克逊是这个家庭的最后一个孩子，比迈克尔小了八岁。

迈克尔的母亲凯瑟琳在西尔斯百货公司兼职。他的父亲约瑟夫[1]在当地一家钢铁厂工作。乔·杰克逊每天只赚三十美元。为了赚更多的钱，他组建了一个叫猎鹰的小乐队，在印第安纳州的酒吧和俱乐部里演奏。乔在乐队中担任吉他手，乐队就在杰克逊家的小房子里练习。

① 约瑟夫（Joseph）的简称为乔（Joe）。

迈克尔的父母都很喜欢音乐。迈克尔的母亲歌声优美，会演奏单簧管和钢琴。音乐是他们家庭生活中很重要的一部分。

乔·杰克逊是一个非常严格的父亲。他有很多规矩。他从来都没让孩子们碰过他的吉他——从来没有！他把吉他放在壁橱里，这样他不在家的时候，孩子们也不会想着去玩它。

有一天，蒂托、杰基和杰曼偷偷溜进壁橱，把吉他拿到了蒂托的房间。蒂托想办法弹奏和弦，迈克尔和他的兄弟们则在一旁看着。蒂托之前就一直在仔细观察父亲的演奏手法。

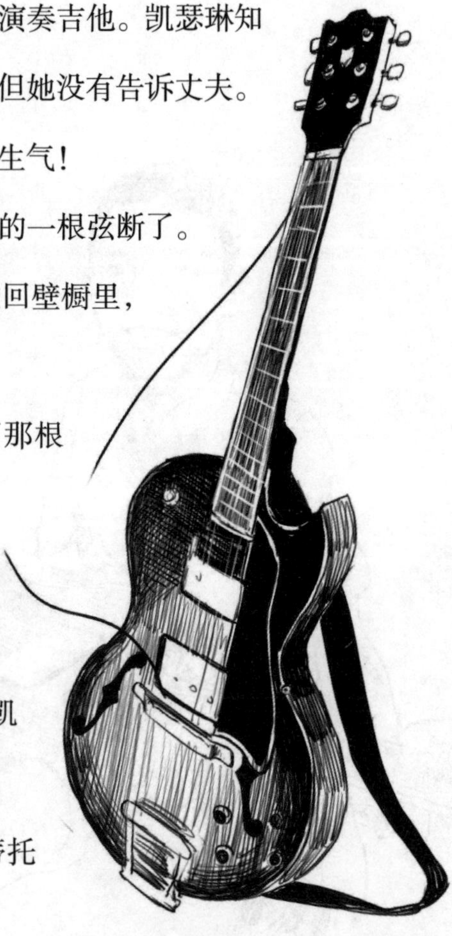

蒂托一点一点地学会了演奏吉他。凯瑟琳知道他偷偷把吉他拿了出来，但她没有告诉丈夫。因为她知道这会让丈夫非常生气！

之后，有一天，吉他上的一根弦断了。蒂托修不好，只能把吉他放回壁橱里，但愿父亲不会注意到。

但不出所料，乔发现了那根断了的弦。父亲很凶，男孩们害怕极了。迈克尔说，乔在孩子们做错事时会打他们一顿。但这一次凯瑟琳站了出来。她告诉乔，孩子们都唱得很好，而且蒂托真的很会弹。

乔把吉他递给蒂托。“让我看看你演奏成什么样。”他说。

当乔看到儿子在演奏方面真的有天分时，他马上就

消气了。他给蒂托带回来一把闪亮的红色吉他。不管在学校里还是放学后，一家人都有音乐课上。很快，杰基、

蒂托、杰曼、马龙和迈克尔组成了一个名叫杰克逊五人组的乐队。

起初杰曼是乐队主唱。迈克尔演奏邦戈鼓。但大家很快意识到，迈克尔才是真正的明日之星。他唱歌富有感情。迈克尔在学校参加才艺比赛时，他的老师在听到他美丽的歌声后潸然泪下。

随着时间的推移，乔·杰克逊决定将所有的一切投入到他儿子们的音乐生涯中。家里虽然没有多少钱，但乔仍然把所有的钱都花在了乐器上。

孩子们每天放学后必须排练，没有时间到外面去玩。如果有人在排练中犯了错误，乔就会惩罚他们。他有时甚至会用皮带打他们！

迈克尔在唱歌方面没犯多少错误，但有一次他在乐队训练中迟到了。有时候他也会违反家里的规矩。乔因为这些事情惩罚了他。乔打迈克尔的时候，迈克尔有时候会反击。他会试图打他父亲！有一次，他向他父亲扔了一只鞋！这个举动让乔更加生气，他打迈克尔打得更重了。

迈克尔讨厌他父亲对待他的方式，但他热爱唱歌和跳舞。他在表演的时候非常开心。

乐队做好了充足的准备后，乔给他们在当地一个名叫“幸运先生”的夜总会里找了份工作，迈克尔在那时仅仅六岁！

到他八岁时，他每周要工作六晚，杰克逊五人组每晚需要完成五场演出，有时在酒吧，有时在夜总会。

迈克尔看到了很多在这个年纪不该看的事情。他每天晚上要很晚才能回家。第二天没有睡够就要去上学。

迈克尔的母亲很担心他。她是一位虔诚的宗教信徒。她带迈克尔去教堂，告诉他永远不要骂脏话，她认为迈克尔不应该在酒吧里鬼混。

但是乔想让儿子们成功的心很坚定。随着乐队变得越来越好，乔开始带他们参加镇上甚至偏远城市的才艺比赛。他们总能赢得胜利。在芝加哥的一场重要才艺比赛中，他们连续三周赢得了胜利。

与此同时，乔决定是时候为乐队出一张唱片了。他们的梦想是去摩城唱片公司。最重要的是，迈克尔和他的哥哥们想要为摩城唱片公司录制音乐。

不管乔尝试了多少次，他都无法让摩城唱片公司的人注意到杰克逊五人组。最后，乔决定，如果他们在纽约市的阿波罗剧院赢下有史以来最大的才艺比赛，摩城

摩城唱片

摩城并不是一个城镇或者城市的名字——它是密歇根州底特律市一家著名唱片公司的名字。这个名字来自底特律的别称“汽车城[1]”，因为这里是汽车的加工厂。摩城唱片公司的音乐结合了灵魂乐和流行音乐，公司里面大部分都是非裔美国人——史蒂维·旺德、诱惑乐队、格拉迪斯·奈特与种子合唱团。他们不管在白人群体还是黑人群体中都很受欢迎。

---

① 底特律的别称为“Motor Town”，意为“汽车城”，底特律以汽车制造业闻名世界，摩城唱片（Motown）便得名于此。

唱片就一定会注意到他们。

阿波罗是一座著名的剧院，地处纽约市哈勒姆区，是非裔美国人的聚居区。

史蒂维·旺德

迈克尔喜爱的歌手都曾在阿波罗剧院表演——像詹姆斯·布朗和史蒂维·旺德。多年来，每周三晚上这里都会举行一场才艺比赛。

所以在1967年夏天，迈克尔九岁那年，乔和他的五个儿子坐上家里的大众面包车，驱车前往纽约。下一站，阿波罗剧院！

这座巨大而辉煌的剧院把迈克尔弄得眼花缭乱，他甚至对这里的麦克风都喜爱有加——它可以从地板上笔直地升起来。舞台附近有一节树干。据说上台前抚摸这节树干可以带来好运。迈克尔和他的哥哥们当然也摸了一把。

但是杰克逊五人组拥有的不只是运气，他们还有天赋。

他们赢下了这场才艺表演。

现在摩城唱片会给他们打电话吗？

回家后，乔·杰克逊定下了一条新规矩。打电话不能超过五分钟。乔不想在摩城唱片打过来时电话占线。

过了几个月，他们没有收到任何摩城唱片的消息。所以乔·杰克逊决定接受一家名为钢城的本地唱片公司的邀请。这家公司只是印第安纳州加里的一个小工作室，但是他们录制了杰克逊五人组的第一首歌。歌曲名叫《大男孩》。这首歌在电台播放，乔还卖出了很多唱片。不过

这种方法并不能让杰克逊五人组出名。

终于，在 1968 年 7 月，摩城唱片的电话来了。迈克尔和他的哥哥们挤进他们的大众面包车，驱车前往底特律。他们准备在唱片公司的负责人贝里 · 戈迪前演唱。如果获得了他的喜爱，他们便可以拿下一份唱片合同!

贝里 · 戈迪

贝里 · 戈迪一听杰克逊兄弟唱歌，便认为迈克尔将会成为一个无与伦比的超级巨星。他告诉他们：“我要让你们这些孩子成为世界上最伟大的人。”他承诺，他们的第一张唱片会成为音乐排行榜上的第一名。

迈克尔 · 杰克逊此时只有十岁——但他正在成长为一个传奇人物。

第二章

加利福尼亚阳光

1969 年，贝里 · 戈迪把摩城唱片搬到了加利福尼亚州的洛杉矶市，杰克逊五人组也和他一起搬来了。戈迪想要他们定居在加利福尼亚州，这样他们就可以在那里录制音乐了。乔和凯瑟琳 · 杰克逊这会儿还在印第安纳州。他们正在收拾房子，准备搬到洛杉矶。

在一段时间里，迈克尔偶尔和贝里 · 戈迪住在一起。剩下的时间，他和一个邻居住在一条街上，这个邻居是一位名叫黛安娜 · 罗斯的著名歌手！

黛安娜 · 罗斯是摩城唱片旗下一个名叫“至高无上”的组合中的明星。她教迈克尔关于艺术和音乐方面的知识，带他去参观博物馆并且教他画画。

迈克尔爱黛安娜 · 罗斯。和她住在一起的时光是他

黛安娜·罗斯

一生中最特殊的时光之一。他也爱加利福尼亚。外面几乎总是阳光明媚，他不敢相信树上居然有橘子。他和他的哥哥们还去了迪士尼乐园。

很快，贝里·戈迪把杰克逊兄弟们带到了新录音室，为他们录了首歌，歌曲名叫《我要你回来》。

贝里·戈迪让孩子们反复录了很多遍，花了好几周才搞定！迈克尔认真听了贝里·戈迪说的每一句话。渐渐地，迈克尔学到了所有音乐行业的知识——他正在向

最优秀的人学习。

贝里·戈迪把杰克逊五人组打造成了流行歌星，给他们买了新衣服，做了新发型。他请人教孩子们如何回答记者的问题，并给孩子们做问答的测试！他们上了餐桌礼仪课。当然，这对迈克尔和他的哥哥们来说不是什么难事。他们的母亲在生活中一直让他们讲礼貌。

《我要你回来》在 1969 年 11 月发行，六周内就卖出了两百万张！正如贝里·戈迪所承诺的那样，他们成了音乐排行榜上的第一名。他们接下来的三首单曲也是第一名。杰克逊五人组成了明星。迈克尔·杰克逊是组合中最有名气的。

他们和黛安娜·罗斯一起做电视节目，还留下了签名。他们还参加了《埃德·沙利文秀》——一个著名的周日晚间电视节目。披头士乐队也曾在这个节目上演出。

他们在纽约麦迪逊广场花园这样的大舞台上举办演唱会。一群狂热的女粉丝尖叫着——迈克尔走到哪里，她们就围到哪里。迈克尔喜欢表演，在舞台上表演是他最快乐的时刻。但他不喜欢被粉丝挤来挤去。有几次女孩们还不小心抓伤了他的脸。太可怕了！

为了避开成群的粉丝，迈克尔还有他的哥哥们大多数时间都躲在酒店的房间里。他们并不自由，但是在一起的时候确实非常开心。他们打恶作剧电话，然后咯咯笑着挂断电话。他们给别的房间点客房服务餐、在走廊里赛跑、打枕头仗。迈克尔喜欢做恶作剧和捉弄别人。他的兄弟们也喜欢这么干。有时候他们还会从酒店窗口朝下面的人扔水球玩！

现在杰克逊一家已经足够富有，能够在加利福尼亚州买下豪宅。乔还有凯瑟琳在好莱坞附近买了一栋房子。一家人在一起生活了很多年。

对迈克尔来说，孩童时期是快乐的时光。尽管他依然无休无止地工作，但是在休息的时候，他至少还能找

点乐子。

但是随着迈克尔逐渐长大，他遇到了青少年都会遇到的问题，不过他跟别的青少年不一样，他的身份是著名歌手。像迈克尔·杰克逊这样的人——拥有财富、名气，万众瞩目——成长会遇到更多困难。

第三章

重大改变

十四岁的时候，迈克尔对自己的长相感到痛苦。他不再是一个可爱的孩子了。粉丝见到他的时候都会惊讶或失望，这事常常发生。有些人甚至认不出来他！他们都想要见到杰克逊五人组专辑封面上的那个人。现在他身材瘦削，还在长个子。

迅猛增高还不是最糟糕的，最糟糕的是他的脸上开始长青春痘。他的爸爸和兄弟一直嘲笑他这一点。他们还嘲笑他的鼻子，说他的鼻子太大了。

迈克尔无法忍受照镜子。甚至洗脸都关着灯，这样他就不用看自己了！

从那时候开始，迈克尔变得十分害羞。他说话轻声细语，不敢直视别人的眼睛。他甚至不想出门去人多的

地方。

对迈克尔的感受，他父亲没有给予足够的尊重。有时候趁迈克尔睡觉的时候，他父亲还会把粉丝带到迈克尔的酒店房间！迈克尔醒来的时候，他的粉丝就在旁边盯着他。

随着时间的推移，迈克尔把越来越多的注意力放在如何变得好看些上。对他来说，变得好看就意味着要想办法遮住他的脸。

其他事情也在改变迈克尔的人生。在长大的过程中，他想要更好地把控自己的音乐，他想要写自己的歌。

迈克尔跟贝里·戈迪说了这事，但是戈迪拒绝了。

所以在1976年的时候，杰克逊一家离开了摩城。这时迈克尔已经快十八岁了。乔和哥伦比亚唱片签下了三百五十万美金的合约，这可不是一笔小数目。最重要的是，迈克尔现在可以写自己的歌，把控唱片的品质。

只有一个问题，那就是杰曼·杰克逊不想离开摩城唱片。他现在已经是个成年人了，而且和贝里·戈迪的女儿结婚了。所以杰曼离开了乐队。兰迪·杰克逊取代了杰曼的位置。从那个时候开始，杰克逊五人组就不能再叫这个名字了。摩城唱片拥有这个名字的所有权。所以他们自称“杰克逊乐队”。

离开贝里·戈迪，迈克尔感觉很遗憾，但是迈克尔

现在是一个聪明的商人了。

两年之后，迈克尔接到了黛安娜·罗斯的一通电话，这让他激动万分。她想要跟他共同出演一部电影。黛安娜即将出演电影《新绿野仙踪》。这部电影的故事以《绿野仙踪》为基础，但是场景设定在纽约市。迈克尔将会扮演稻草人的角色。他很开心，因为他需要化很厚的妆，这可以遮住他的青春痘。他也喜欢在电影里跳舞。

黛安娜发牢骚说迈克尔学舞学得太快，让别人看起来很迟钝。他难以自制，一跳起舞，他便光芒难掩。

《新绿野仙踪》没有大卖，事实上可以说票房惨淡。但是迈克尔享受这部电影的拍摄过程。现在，这成了他梦想的一部分——成为一位电影明星。

在《新绿野仙踪》的片场，迈克尔结交了一个朋友，这个朋友在很多事情上改变了他的人生，他就是昆西·琼斯。

昆西·琼斯

弗雷德·阿斯泰尔（1899—1987）

弗雷德·阿斯泰尔是迈克尔·杰克逊最喜爱的电影明星之一。阿斯泰尔也是美国相当著名的舞者。他跳踢踏舞，动作像芭蕾舞演员一样优雅。他拍摄了很多带有精彩的舞蹈场景的电影。在一部电影中，弗雷德·阿斯泰尔在一面墙上跳舞，然后又在天花板上跳舞！

迈克尔学习了弗雷德·阿斯泰尔的舞蹈动作。在写自传的时候，迈克尔在书的最前面写道："这本书献给弗雷德·阿斯泰尔。"

迈克尔在电视上表演了月球漫步的第二天，他接到了弗雷德·阿斯泰尔的电话，他打电话是为了夸赞迈克尔真的很会跳舞！

昆西和贝里·戈迪一样，是一位出色的唱片制作人，但是昆西不在摩城唱片工作，他自立门户。他像贝里一样，对迈克尔很好，给了他很多帮助。有一天，在电影片场，昆西听到迈克尔读错了一个单词。他很快告诉迈克尔怎么正确发音，迈克尔十分感激。从那时开始，这两个人就成了朋友，昆西就如迈克尔的父亲一般。

现在对迈克尔来说，是一个完美的时机。既然已经离开了摩城，他便准备在音乐领域做出一些改变。昆西·琼斯就是那个帮他实现这些改变的人。

1979年8月，迈克尔推出了一张独唱专辑，由昆西制作。这张专辑的名字叫《墙外》。昆西说服了其他巨星来为这张专辑写歌。披头士的成员保罗·麦卡特尼就写了其中一首歌。

保罗·麦卡特尼

在同月，迈克尔过了二十一岁生日。他现在已经足够成熟，能够做所有的决定了。

他的第一个决定就十分重大，他决定开除自己的经纪人。他的经纪人就是他的父亲！迈克尔知道他的父亲一开始为家庭做了很多，他创立了杰克逊五人组，把他们带到了摩城唱片公司。

但是迈克尔不想让乔再管理他的生活。从现在起，迈克尔要自己做主——没有人能够指挥他做任何事。

第四章

名声与财富

约翰·布兰卡

既然乔已经不再管理迈克尔的事业了，迈克尔需要找一位脑子灵光的经纪人来帮助他。他雇的第一个人是一位律师，名字叫约翰·布兰卡。接下来的几年中，布兰卡从唱片公司帮迈克尔争取到了给歌手的最大利益。

迈克尔与哥伦比亚公司合作的第一张个人专辑大获成功。专辑中的四首歌都进入了音乐榜单的前十位。在 1980 年，迈克尔获得了格莱美奖——音乐行业的最高荣誉。

但是他开心吗？

不，迈克尔并不开心，因为他只拿到了一个格莱美奖。

迈克尔很沮丧，因为这个奖是颁给最佳 R&B 男歌手的。“R&B”的意思是“节奏布鲁斯”。大部分 R&B 歌手是非裔美国人。迈克尔感觉格莱美仿佛在说：“就黑人歌手来说，这是张不错的专辑。但是相比其他流行音乐歌手来说，这还不够好。”

迈克尔决定下次拿下年度最佳专辑奖。

迈克尔在 1982 年进录音棚，开始录制新的歌曲，昆西担任制作人。他录了四首自己写的歌。还有一首歌是二重唱，保罗·麦卡特尼跟他一起唱。这首歌的名字叫《这个女孩是我的》。

这张名为《战栗》的专辑一炮而红。迈克尔写的两首歌《比利·琼》和《避开》均冲上了排行榜冠军的宝

座。另一首由别人写的专辑同名单曲《战栗》也冲上了榜首。

不久，《战栗》成了有史以来最畅销的专辑。发行一年，也就是 1983 年，销量就达到一千万张。没有一张专辑比《战栗》更畅销。在短短四年里，迈克尔就赚了一亿九千万美元。

是什么让《战栗》大获成功呢？有很多因素。第一，昆西和迈克尔配合完美，给音乐注入了活力。第二，迈克尔正处在艺人的巅峰时期。在音乐行业深耕了十九年，他已经成为一位专家。他知道他需要慢慢来——就像贝里 · 戈迪说过的那样——一遍一遍地录制歌曲，直到完美。

有时候迈克尔会通宵记歌词，第二天，他们会关掉录音棚的灯，在黑暗中录歌，这让迈克尔沉浸在私密的氛围中，因此他可以将自己所有的情绪和感受都融入歌曲中。

迈克尔和昆西花了几个月的时间录制专辑。他们一遍一遍地混音，直到音乐听起来是他们想要的感觉。

专辑《战栗》成功的另外一个原因是里面的音乐视

频，迈克尔把它们当成微电影去构想。他把所有的精力和才能都投入了进去。首先就是为单曲《比利·琼》拍摄视频。

起初，迈克尔无法在电视上播放他的视频。

为什么呢？

一个仅成立一年的音乐视频频道全球音乐电视台，认为观众只想看白人表演者。

哥伦比亚唱片公司的总裁打电话给全球音乐电视台。他发出了警告，如果不播放迈克尔·杰克逊的视频，就不再允许他们播放哥伦比亚公司白人明星如布鲁斯·斯普林斯廷和比利·乔尔的音乐视频。

全球音乐电视台妥协了，他们播放了《比利·琼》的视频。一播出便一鸣惊人，一时间《战栗》成了所有

布鲁斯·斯普林斯廷

榜单——不止“黑人音乐”榜单——的榜首。

迈克尔还为《战栗》这张专辑制作了另外两个无与伦比的视频。第一个是单曲《避开》的音乐视频。视频内容是关于街头帮派的。迈克尔邀请了洛杉矶真正的街头帮派成员出演。

他最精彩、最浩大、最昂贵的音乐电影是为专辑同名单曲《战栗》拍摄的。迈克尔想要呈现的效果是自己变成狼人。他邀请了一位恐怖电影的导演。视频里甚至还有他和僵尸跳舞的场景。

在这年的格莱美上，迈克尔凭借《战栗》这张专辑取得了十二个提名。他开心极了，在家里欢呼、尖叫、舞动。

格莱美之夜，他获得了八个奖。《避开》获得了年度最佳唱片奖，《战栗》获得了年度最佳专辑奖。

不久后，迈克尔被邀请到白宫与罗纳德·里根总统会面。这是否足够让迈克尔·杰克逊感到快乐呢？他是否会为自己的成功感到满足呢？

迈克尔有绝对音感吗?

绝对音感是指人仅仅通过耳朵听就能分辨所有音符的能力。

迈克尔·杰克逊没有接受过识谱训练，所以他不能说出那些音符。但是他的音可以像拥有绝对音感的人一样准。迈克尔从来没走过调，别人

走调了会让他抓狂。

有一次，滚石乐队的米克·贾格尔和迈克尔合唱的时候跑调了。迈克尔就不想再跟他合唱了。他说米克唱得平平无奇！

昆西·琼斯的录音师说迈克尔·杰克逊是为数不多的在录音室里不需要修音的歌手。他的表现永远那么完美。

第五章

伤痕累累

专辑《战栗》发布之后，迈克尔·杰克逊成了世界上最出名的流行音乐明星。

然而，他的内心深处还藏有深深的悲伤。也许是不快乐的童年遗留下来的。他感觉很孤独，仿佛没有人能够理解他。

对外界来说，迈克尔就像一位巨星。在舞台上，他身着华丽的服饰。全球的粉丝都想要模仿他。他最出名的演出服之一就是一件军夹克，上面有金色的穗带和闪烁的人造钻石，珠宝。他的头发长且卷曲。他经常戴墨镜。

但内心深处，他依然十分腼腆，对自己的样貌也不够自信。迈克尔患有皮肤病，需要很多化妆品才能遮住，

而且他还使用皮肤漂白霜[1]。

他已经做了两次鼻子整形手术，整鼻子就是做手术让鼻子小一点。

① 此处有争议。

在 1984 年 1 月，迈克尔发生了一场意外。他正在洛杉矶的一个大礼堂里为百事可乐拍广告。观众中有一大群粉丝，他本该走下舞台的台阶，但火花和烟花在他身边炸开了。突然，他的头发着火了。

一开始，迈克尔没有意识到发生了什么。他还在舞动、旋转着，然后他用手猛地摸了摸自己的脑袋。

迈克尔被紧急送往医院。他烧伤严重，不得不做手术。他的头皮再也回不到以前的样子了。之后，医生便给他开药来止痛。

在那之前，迈克尔·杰克逊从来没有吸过毒，但是他服用了医生给他开的止痛药，时间长了，他对这些药品成瘾，停不下来了。

但是，百事可乐广告意外事件给他带来两件好事。百事可乐公司捐赠了一百五十万美元给接诊迈克尔的烧伤中心。

百事可乐公司还给了迈克尔一份超过五百二十万美元的合同，请他来为百事公司拍摄更多广告。约翰·布兰卡帮迈克尔谈下了这份合同。迈克尔已经十分出名，并且受到众人喜爱。不过现在，他即将成为音乐界最富有的人。

第六章

收购披头士的音乐版权

迈克尔在音乐行业深耕多年，已经知道游戏规则——经常是唱片公司赚得盆满钵满，而歌手和作曲人只能拿蝇头小利。为什么呢？大部分的钱都来自歌曲的版权。当然，歌手每卖出一张唱片就能拿到一定的报酬，但经常是卖出一张唱片只能拿到几分钱，甚至更少。这种方式不可能让他们变得富有。

杰克逊五人组从来没有拥有过他们歌曲的版权，其中一个原因是这些歌曲不是他们写的，而且贝里·戈迪跟所有的歌手都签订了合同，规定所有歌曲为摩城唱片所有。

披头士也面临一样的处境。他们写了很多好歌，但是他们都没有版权。披头士从唱片和演唱会门票的销售中赚了很多钱，还从电影和电视中赚钱。但是他们却没拥有自己歌曲的版权，这才是赚大钱的地方。

1981 年，迈克尔和保罗·麦卡特尼见面时，保罗告诉了迈克尔一个秘密——他正在收购其他歌手畅销作品的版权。保罗列出了他已经收购的歌曲名单。他说这是他的目录。他通过拿下别人的版权来挣钱。保罗表示迈克尔也应该这么做。所以迈克尔询问了自己的律师约翰·布兰卡，让他关注一下可以收购的歌曲。

1984年的一天，布兰卡说有一个新的歌曲目录要出售——披头士的歌！迈克尔不敢相信，他想要拿下这个歌曲目录，不管这要花费多大代价。

但是这并不容易。万一保罗·麦卡特尼想要买回他自己的歌呢？

约翰·布兰卡问了保罗·麦卡特尼的律师，保罗是否有这样的计划？律师表示没有——实在是太贵了。但是保罗没有意识到是迈克尔·杰克逊想要买下披头士的歌，如果他知道的话，也许会改变想法。

布兰卡为这些歌出价三千万美元。其他人出价更高，价格水涨船高。很快，一些纽约和好莱坞最聪明的人告诉迈克尔，他这样太疯狂了。他花的钱实在多得离谱。

迈克尔没有听他们的。布兰卡花了几个月的时间，终于赢下了这场竞价战。迈克尔花了四千七百五十万美元买下了披头士的歌。

事实表明，买下披头士的歌是迈克尔做出的最明智的事情。不到十年，这些歌曲价值就达到一亿五千万美元，每年给迈克尔带来一千万美元的收入。现在，价值已经达到十亿美元啦！

保罗·麦卡特尼对此感觉懊恼，他打电话给迈克尔，想聊聊这件事，毕竟他们是朋友。

保罗说，和迈克尔和杰克逊五人组一样，披头士在年轻的时候也没有得到应得的利益，既然现在迈克尔有这些歌的所有权，他是否考虑给披头士更大的利润分成呢？

迈克尔表示拒绝。尽管迈克尔声音柔和，性格内敛，但他在生意方面十分强硬。对他来说，这就是一笔生意而已。

《天下一家》

1985年，迈克尔和莱昂内尔·里奇写了一首叫《天下一家》的歌来做慈善。这首歌所赚的钱都用于帮助埃塞俄比亚和苏丹这样的非洲国家的饥饿人口。

昆西·琼斯制作了这张唱片。他召集了一群知名歌星齐聚录音棚。鲍勃·迪伦也在其中。还有布鲁斯·斯普林斯廷、史蒂维·旺德、蒂

娜·特纳、比利·乔尔、辛迪·劳帕、雷·查尔斯、黛安娜·罗斯等。当然，迈克尔·杰克逊和莱昂内尔·里奇也有独唱部分。

这张唱片卖了数百万张，并且拿下了三个格莱美奖，录制的过程也被记录在音乐视频当中，轰动一时。这首歌募集了六千三百万美元善款，这些钱都用于购买食物、衣服还有药品。

第七章

怪人杰克

有了这些财富，迈克尔几乎可以做他想做的任何事情。没有人可以阻止他做任何事情——至少他的家人和朋友不敢。有时候布兰卡会告诫迈克尔谨言慎行，但是即使如此，迈克尔还是会义无反顾地遵从自己内心的想法。

好多迈克尔想做的事情看起来十分疯狂。

1986 年，迈克尔去了一家医院，看见了一个玻璃箱子——像是一个透明棺材，那叫高压氧舱，是给那些需要额外氧气的病人用的。他躺进这个箱子，拍了一张照片，然后把这张照片寄到报社。他说，他每晚都睡在里面，这样他就能活到一百五十岁。

这不是真的，他只是在开玩笑。他读了一本书，是

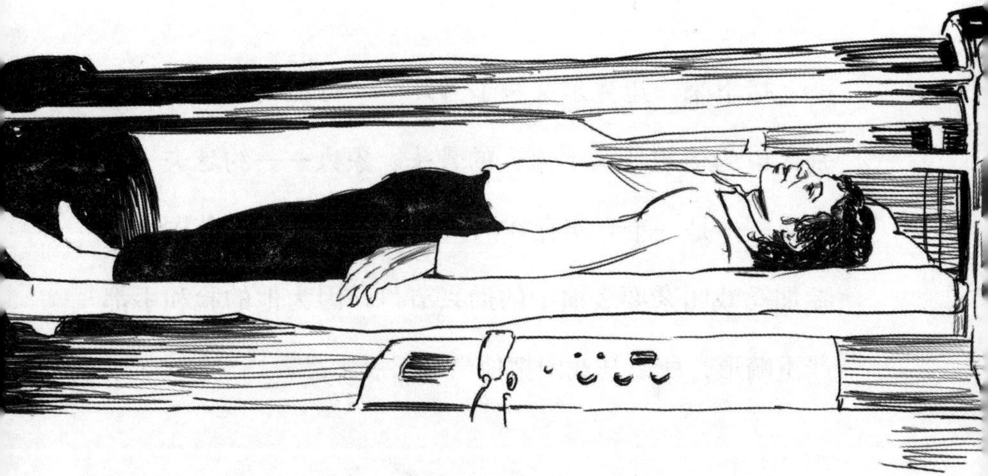

著名的马戏团老板菲尼亚斯·泰勒·巴纳姆写的。巴纳姆写道，没有所谓的“坏名声”。迈克尔觉得他说得对。

菲尼亚斯·泰勒·巴纳姆

接下来，迈克尔又编了另外一个奇怪的故事。他让别人以为他想要买下象人的骨头。象人——约瑟夫·梅里克——是一个真实存在的人，19 世纪生活在英国。他参加马戏团杂耍表演中的助兴节目，因为他的脸和手都严重畸形，所以马戏团把他当成了展示品。

报社人员听说此事，都觉得迈克尔·杰克逊疯了。一家报纸称他为“怪人杰克”。这个绰号一直沿用至今。

1988年，迈克尔养了一只黑猩猩宠物，名叫“泡泡”。他跟别人说他与黑猩猩共进晚餐。

迈克尔现在有名有利，但是他并没有比以前更快乐。他依然讨厌自己的长相，一直在脸上整容。最后，因为整了太多次，他的鼻尖都快要消失了！

迈克尔还在自己的下巴处做了一个窝。手术后，下巴还没有愈合，他便用外科口罩遮住伤口。但是有些人觉得迈克尔就是疯了，而且害怕细菌。

迈克尔在一些照片里看起来非常奇怪。报纸上一直称他为“怪人杰克”。迈克尔对此感觉很伤心，但是他之前都在试图用错误的方式来寻求关注。现在他后悔了，他想要尽可能地远离公众视野。

1988 年，他找到了一个可以藏身的好地方。他在加利福尼亚州的圣巴巴拉县买下了一个“梦幻庄园”。面积近三千英亩[①]——比大多数大城市里的公园大得多。

① 英美制面积单位。1 英亩 = 4046.86 平方米。

对迈克尔来说，梦幻庄园圆了他的梦。这是他的一个私人乐园！这里有摩天轮、小火车、碰碰车、海盗船、过山车、宠物乐园等。儿童雕塑随处可见。野生动物四处闲逛。一个巨大的室外时钟像一栋楼那么大，周围是用鲜花拼成的“梦幻庄园”字样。当然，里面还有游泳池、电影院，还收藏了大量电子游戏。迈克尔还为自己建了一栋大房子，还有一栋小一点的宾客房。

迈克尔从未拥有真正的童年——他五岁便开始工作。在梦幻庄园里，他可以整日玩耍。这简直完美，只不过，谁会跟他一起享受这些快乐呢?

迈克尔依然爱着自己的家人，但是他不想再和他们继续生活。他觉得家人经常对他要求过多，他们希望他能回到杰克逊乐队做巡回演唱会，迈克尔不想这样。

所以迈克尔一个人搬进了梦幻庄园。这是一个私人领域，四周围着大门。大多数时间，迈克尔·杰克逊都是独自一人。

麻烦事

迈克尔喜欢和孩子待在一起。不论何时，他都会想办法友善、慷慨地对待他们。有时候他会去医院拜访生病的孩子，还会邀请他们及他们的家人来梦幻庄园。他买了大包大包的玩具，然后花上几个小时给玩具装上电池。他把这些玩具送给那些来演唱会后台看他的孩子们。

时间长了，迈克尔和几个年轻的男孩成了亲密的朋友。有些人会说迈克尔和他们走得太近了。有时候迈克尔会带着男孩们去巡演。

慢慢地，有一个男孩的父母变得有些担心。这个男孩说，迈克尔用一种不适宜的方式与他发生了肢体接触。1993 年，警方介入，事情在报纸上发酵。迈克尔否认了所有事情。他说这个家长只是想要从他这里讹钱，用撒谎来达到目的。最终迈克尔给这一家人赔偿了上百万美元，他们才撤销对他的起诉。

几年之后，又有一个男孩说迈克尔对他有不当的肢体接触。这一次，迈克尔不得不走上法庭，但是很多迈克尔的年轻朋友都站在了他那一边，并且为他说话。他们说迈克尔从来没有对他们做过什么不好的事情。在审判的最后，他无罪释放。在他的余生中，迈克尔坚持说他没有做错什么。

第八章

自己的家

迈克尔不怎么约会。有一小段时间，他和塔特姆·奥尼尔约过会。她之前是个童星，而且是一位电影演员的女儿。迈克尔喜欢塔特姆，是因为她知道在演艺行业当童星是怎样的。

塔特姆·奥尼尔

几年后，他和波姬·小丝开始约会。她也是因当儿童模特和儿童演员而出名的。在那之后，他就没有找过女朋友了。

波姬·小丝

但是当他人生出现麻烦时，他希望有人可以帮助他，理解他。他感觉万分孤独。他和黛安娜·罗斯失去了联系。他开始服用药品——处方药，但是他服用过量。他需要帮助。

莉萨·玛丽·普雷斯利

迈克尔打给了他的朋友莉萨·玛丽·普雷斯利。她是首位摇滚巨星埃尔维斯·普雷斯利的女儿。迈克尔和她是很多年的朋友。

迈克尔在外面巡演的时候，他们常通电话。有一天，迈克尔在电话里问她是否愿意嫁给他。莉萨在那个时候已经跟别人结了婚。但是她还是答应了。她离婚了之后可以和他结婚。

1994 年 5 月 26 日，迈克尔和莉萨·玛丽在加勒比海的多米尼加共和国举办了秘密婚礼。关于这场婚礼，迈克尔甚至没有告诉他的妈妈。莉萨也没有告诉她的家人。

他们回到美国后，几个月内，莉萨和迈克尔都没有

王和流行音乐之王

埃尔维斯·普雷斯利是第一位摇滚巨星。就像迈克尔·杰克逊一样，他以独特的舞台表演出名。他也拍摄电影，并且在表演中身着华丽的服装。在20世纪50年代的时候，年轻姑娘们爱他，小伙子们想要成为他。他非常有名，别人都称他为“王”。

迈克尔·杰克逊也想要有一个这样的称呼。他想要像埃尔维斯那样出名。1988年，全球音乐电视台邀请迈克尔出席他们的音乐视频颁奖典礼。他同意了，但是有一个前提，那就是从此以后，全球音乐电视台每次提到他，都要称他为“流行音乐之王”。这种方法奏效了——从那时起，大家都用这个光鲜的名号来称呼他。

透露他们结婚的事。迈克尔知道，这个秘密泄露出去后，会有很多曝光度——他想得没错。

这场婚姻持续了不到两年。令婚姻失败的一个原因可能是迈克尔想要孩子，但是莉萨已经有了孩子，他们在 1996 年离婚，但是他们在那之后做了很多年的朋友。

黛比 · 罗

迈克尔想要孩子的想法很坚定，如果莉萨不能跟他有孩子的话，迈克尔会找另一个愿意跟他生的人。他找了另外一个朋友，这个朋友是一个护士，名字叫黛比 · 罗。迈克尔是在看皮肤科医生的时候遇到她的。迈克尔和黛比一直保持通话联系。当黛比同意跟迈克尔生孩子，并且愿意把孩子给他的时候，他激动万分。

他给了她很多钱，并且给她买了几百万的房子。对黛比即便不是他的妻子还愿意跟他生孩子这件事，他十分感激。

但是迈克尔的母亲对此并不认同。当凯瑟琳发现黛比已经怀孕的时候，她希望迈克尔能够和黛比结婚。迈克尔一直敬爱并且尊重他的母亲。他知道母亲是虔诚的宗教信徒。在这件事情上，他无法拒绝他的母亲。

所以，在 11 月 13 日的时候，迈克尔和黛比在澳大利亚的一家酒店里结了婚。大概有十五个朋友出席了婚礼，黛比和迈克尔都身着黑色服装。

1997年2月13日。黛比产下了一个男婴。迈克尔给他取名为普林斯·迈克尔·杰克逊[1]。大家都说这个名字太夸张了。迈克尔是不是觉得自己的孩子有皇室血统呢？并不是。实际上，迈克尔的祖父和曾祖父都叫普林斯，这是他们家族的名字。

迈克尔一个人带着这个孩子回到了梦幻庄园，没有和黛比一起。由一群保姆和护士照看这个孩子。黛比从来没有和迈克尔生活过，她不像是孩子的母亲。

1998年4月3日，黛比和迈克尔又生下了一个孩

① 普林斯（Prince）意为“王子”。

子，这次是个女婴，他们给她取名帕里斯，全名叫帕里斯·凯瑟琳·迈克尔·杰克逊。

跟之前一样，迈克尔独自一人抚养这个孩子。黛比没有参与，只是看望过孩子几次。最后，黛比决定不再和迈克尔维持婚姻关系，在 1999 年，两人办理离婚。

几年之后，迈克尔对世界宣称自己已经有了第三个孩子。这一次，孩子的妈妈不是黛比，迈克尔也没有透露孩子的母亲是谁。这个男婴出生于2002年2月21日。迈克尔给他取名为普林斯·迈克尔二世，绰号叫“毯毯”。从此，迈克尔的大儿子也被称为普林斯·迈克尔一世。

现在如他所愿，迈克尔拥有了一个家。他的生活会变得更简单吗？前方会有快乐等待他吗？

很可惜，答案是否定的。

第九章

为时已晚

20世纪80年代末到90年代初，迈克尔一直在录制动人的音乐。他的专辑《真棒》在1987年问世，销量达到数百万张。这张专辑里有一首歌叫《镜中人》，虽然这首歌不是他写的，但是这是迈克尔最喜欢的歌之一。这首歌讲述的是通过改变自己来改变世界。迈克尔把这首歌挣到的所有钱都捐给了一个癌症儿童夏令营。

四年后，迈克尔的下一张专辑《危险之旅》发布。这张专辑里包含了他最有趣的歌曲之一——《黑与白》。歌词讲的是，人是黑色皮肤还是白色皮肤都无关紧要。这首歌的音乐视频展示了几十张不同肤色的人脸，它们相互变化或融合。歌曲发行的第一天，几乎所有美国排名前四十的广播电台都播放了这首歌。

迈克尔依然是一位才华横溢、富有创造力的巨星。但是他的个人生活依然不尽如人意。他又开始服用处方药了。

到 2005 年，他已经好几年没有出过一张大热专辑了。他没有出去巡演。他的一些经理认为，他是担心他的演出不够好。如果演出不够精彩，迈克尔认为他会让粉丝失望。

有几年，迈克尔和他的孩子居住在国外。他们在中东的巴林生活了很长时间，然后又搬到爱尔兰，最后他们搬回了美国，住在内华达州的拉斯维加斯。一直以来，迈克尔都像超级巨星一样大手大脚地花钱。每年，他花

迈克尔在拉斯维加斯的房子

的钱是他赚的钱的两倍。

2007 年，迈克尔陷入了严重的财务危机。他借了很多钱来维持他奢侈的生活方式，但是他需要尽快偿还他的债务，那可能意味着他将失去一切——包括披头士的歌曲以及他的梦幻庄园。

迈克尔不得不重新开始工作。他需要办大型演唱会，并且录制大热专辑。所以他同意举办一系列演唱会，主题为《就是这样》。从 2009 年开始，在伦敦会先后举办五十场。

第一场演唱会开始的几周里，迈克尔无休止地排练。有时他觉得这感觉很好，很享受。他依然是一位优秀的歌手和舞者。伴唱歌手经常在一旁观看并且鼓掌，但是

迈克尔担心得要命。他依然追求完美。万一他不能给他的粉丝呈现精彩的演出呢？他晚上都会担心得整夜无法入睡。

迈克尔再一次寻求药物。为了更好地入睡，迈克尔雇了一个叫康拉德·默里的医生。医生只应该做有利于病人的事情，但是默里医生没有做到这点。他给迈克尔注射了一种药，这种药在医院里是给做手术的人用的。这种药十分危险，能让迈克尔一夜昏睡，这正是迈克尔想要的。

康拉德·默里医生

2009 年 6 月 25 日，迈克尔·杰克逊死于过量使用这些药。默里医生被指控意外杀死了他。因为这个罪行，他坐了两年牢。

当大家听说迈克尔·杰克逊去世时，世界各地的上百万粉丝十分震惊和伤心。洛杉矶举行了一场盛大的追思会，并在电视上播出。葬礼上，很多人发了言，包括贝里·戈迪。黛安娜·罗斯也送来了她的悼词，在会上由人朗读。迈克尔的女儿帕里斯也讲了话，表达了对父亲的爱和思念。巨星歌手们演唱了曲目，来纪念迈克尔。迈克尔的每个兄弟都戴了一只镶有亮片的白手套，来纪念迈克尔。他们和包括迈克尔父母在内的其他家人一起坐在前排。

仪式上有一个环节，杰曼·杰克逊演唱了迈克尔最喜欢的一首歌《微笑》。歌词可能说明了很多关于迈克尔大部分时间的感受，歌词是：“微笑吧，尽管心痛。微笑吧，即使心碎。”

迈克尔已经去世，人们便想要记住迈克尔的美好。他天赋极高，是送给世界上几百万人的礼物。他的歌曲

和舞蹈给人带来了很多快乐。可惜的是，表演似乎是他寻找快乐的唯一方式。

他去世的时候仅仅五十岁，但是已经成了传奇人物。其实，在葬礼上，贝里·戈迪说“流行音乐之王”这个名号对迈克尔来说不够响亮。他说迈克尔·杰克逊是史上最伟大的艺人。

杰克逊乐队——他们现在在哪儿?

迈克尔去世之后，杰克逊乐队在全世界举办了演唱会来纪念迈克尔。

杰曼·杰克逊的唱片事业也很成功。他推出了自己的个人唱片，并且在1980年获得了格莱美奖。他还和著名歌手惠特尼·休斯敦录制了双人合唱。

杰基、蒂托、兰迪这些年都是作为音乐家在别人的专辑中表演。

迈克尔的妹妹们都有自己的事业。拉托亚录制了专辑，并出现在电视真人秀节目中。

珍妮特·杰克逊本身就是一位巨星。她的个人专辑销售了数百万张，她在超级碗演出，在电视和电影中都曾露面。

迈克尔·杰克逊生平年表

1958 年 — 迈克尔·杰克逊出生在印第安纳州的加里。
1967 年 — 杰克逊五人组在哈勒姆区的阿波罗剧院演出，赢下了才艺比赛。
— 与钢城唱片公司签下第一张唱片的合约。
1968 年 — 杰克逊五人组与摩城唱片公司签约。
1969 年 — 迈克尔和家人移居加利福尼亚州。
1970 年 — 杰克逊五人组在一年内打造三首热门单曲。
1976 年 — 杰克逊五人组离开摩城唱片公司，与哥伦比亚唱片公司签约。
1978 年 — 与黛安娜·罗斯一同出演《新绿野仙踪》。
1979 年 — 推出个人专辑《墙外》，由昆西·琼斯制作。
1983 年 — 在摩城二十五周年庆典上表演月球漫步。
— 专辑《战栗》发布并且成为有史以来最畅销的专辑。
1984 年 — 赢得八个格莱美奖。
— 在百事可乐广告拍摄过程中烧伤。
— 收购披头士的音乐。
1985 年 — 创作并录制《天下一家》。
1988 年 — 买下梦幻庄园。
1994 年 — 和莉萨·玛丽·普雷斯利结婚。
1996 年 — 和莉萨·玛丽·普雷斯利离婚，与黛比·罗结婚。
1997 年 — 第一个儿子出生，取名普林斯·迈克尔·杰克逊。
1998 年 — 女儿出生，取名帕里斯·凯瑟琳·迈克尔·杰克逊。
2002 年 — 第二个儿子出生，取名普林斯·迈克尔二世。
2005 年 — 接受审判，被判无罪。
2009 年 — 五十岁去世。

世界大事记

1957 年 —《西区故事》在美国首映。

1962 年 — 约翰·格伦成为第一个绕地球飞行的美国人。

1963 年 — 马丁·路德·金发表演讲《我有一个梦想》。

— 约翰·肯尼迪被刺杀。

1964 年 — 纳尔逊·曼德拉在南非被判处终身监禁。

— 披头士乐队首次出现在《埃德·沙利文秀》上。

1967 年 — 瑟古德·马歇尔成为第一位黑人最高法院大法官。

1968 年 — 马丁·路德·金被刺杀。

1970 年 — 披头士乐队宣布解散。

1971 年 — 美国宪法第二十六修正案将投票年龄降到十八岁。

1974 年 — 理查德·尼克松成为第一位辞职的美国总统。

1977 年 — 埃尔维斯·普雷斯利去世。

1979 年 — 玛格丽特·撒切尔成为英国第一位女首相。

1981 年 — 全球音乐电视台首次亮相。

1982 年 — 首张 CD 唱片发行。

1986 年 —《奥普拉·温弗里秀》在国家电视台播出。

1989 年 — 分隔东西柏林的柏林墙被推倒。

1994 年 — 纳尔逊·曼德拉成为南非总统。

2001 年 — 苹果公司推出 iPod。

2009 年 — 巴拉克·奥巴马成为美国总统。

Who Was Michael Jackson?

Pasadena, California.

Michael Jackson edged over to the side of the stage during a concert in 1983. He had purchased a spy hat, just like one in his latest music video. Michael had an idea for how to use the hat during the song he was going to sing—and he really hoped it would work.

The concert at the Pasadena Civic Auditorium was going to be broadcast on TV. Fifty million people would watch it. Many other famous singers had already performed. Now it was time for Michael's solo number.

Michael Jackson was already one of the biggest pop stars in the world. But he was never satisfied. He wanted to do something onstage no one would ever forget. He wanted the audience to go crazy!

As soon as the music started, Michael put on the hat and began to dance. Instantly, the audience jumped to its feet. They screamed and cheered. They recognized the hat and knew the song was "Billie Jean."

Wearing a sparkly black jacket, a silver shirt, and one white glove, Michael did dance moves that no one had ever seen before! He had practiced them in his kitchen the night before. His legs twitched. His hips jerked. His foot thumped. He threw the hat offstage in a smooth move that made the audience go wild again.

And then, in the middle of the song, he did something amazing. He slid backward, while making it look like he was walking forward. He called it the Moonwalk! The Moonwalk only lasted five seconds, but it was magical.

By the end of the song, everyone was standing. The crowd was cheering. His whole family kissed him when he came offstage. No one would ever forget that Moonwalk. In fact, it became Michael Jackson's most famous move.

But was Michael happy? Not completely. He was thrilled that people loved the show. But he thought his dance could have been better. He hadn't stayed up on his toes long enough after the big spin at the end of the Moonwalk.

For Michael Jackson, nothing was ever good enough. He always wanted to be perfect. That's what made him work so hard to achieve his dreams—to become the best-selling singer of all time. That's what drove him to become the King of Pop.

Chapter 1

Small House, Big Dreams

Michael Joseph Jackson was born in Gary, Indiana, on August 29, 1958. The Jackson house was tiny and already crowded. Michael had four older brothers and two sisters. Maureen, called Rebbie, was the oldest. Next came Jackie, then Tito, Jermaine, LaToya, and Marlon. A few years after Michael was born, Randy came along. Janet Jackson was the baby of the family, born eight years after Michael.

Michael's mother, Katherine, worked part-time at a Sears department store. His father, Joseph, worked at a local steel mill. Joe Jackson earned only thirty dollars a day. To make extra money, he had a small band called the Falcons. They played in local bars and clubs around Indiana. Joe played guitar, and the band practiced in the Jacksons' small house.

Both of Michael's parents had always loved music. His mother sang and played the clarinet and piano. Music was a big part of family life.

Joe Jackson was a very strict father. He had lots of rules. None of the kids were allowed to touch his guitar—ever! He kept it in a closet so they wouldn't be tempted to play it when he wasn't home.

One day, Tito, Jackie, and Jermaine sneaked into the closet and took the guitar to Tito's room. Michael and his brothers watched as Tito figured out how to play chords. Tito had been studying their father carefully.

Little by little, Tito taught himself how to play. Katherine knew he was sneaking the guitar out, but she didn't tell her husband. She knew how mad he would be!

Then, one day, one of the strings on the guitar broke. Tito couldn't fix it, so he just put the guitar back in the closet and hoped his father wouldn't notice.

Of course Joe saw the broken string. All the boys were terrified, because their father could be so mean. Michael said that Joe hit the kids when they did something wrong. But this time Katherine spoke up. She told Joe that the boys were good singers—and that Tito could really play.

Joe handed Tito the guitar. "Let me see what you can do," he said.

As soon as Joe saw that his sons had talent, he wasn't angry. He brought home a shiny red guitar for Tito. Everyone in the family got music lessons, either at school or after school. Pretty soon, Jackie, Tito, Jermaine, Marlon, and Michael formed a band. They would become the Jackson 5.

At first Jermaine was the lead singer. Michael played the bongo drums. But it didn't take long for everyone to realize that Michael was the real star. He sang with so much feeling. When Michael entered a talent contest at school, his teachers cried at the sound of his beautiful voice.

As time went by, Joe Jackson decided to put everything into his sons' music careers. The family didn't have much money, but Joe spent all they had on musical instruments.

The Jackson boys had to rehearse every single day after school. There was no time to go outside or play. If anyone made a mistake while rehearsing, Joe punished them. Sometimes he hit them with his belt!

Michael didn't make many mistakes singing. But one time he was late for band practice. Sometimes he broke the rules around the house, too. Joe punished him for those things. When Joe hit Michael, sometimes Michael fought back. He would try to punch his father! Once, he threw a shoe at him! That made Joe madder still, and he beat Michael all the more.

Michael hated the way his father treated him, but he loved singing and dancing. He was happy when he was performing.

When the band was ready, Joe got them a job at a local

nightclub called Mr. Lucky's. Michael was only six years old at the time!

By the time he was eight years old, he was working six nights a week. The Jackson 5 had to play five shows every night. Sometimes they played in bars or nightclubs.

Michael saw a lot of things he was too young to see. He got home late each night, too. He barely got enough sleep to go to school the next day.

Michael's mother worried about him. She was a very religious person. She had taken Michael to church and taught him never to swear. She didn't think he should be hanging out in bars.

But Joe was determined to make his sons a success. As the band got better, Joe started entering them in talent contests around town and even in distant cities. They always won. In Chicago, they won an important talent contest three weeks in a row.

Meanwhile, Joe decided it was time for the band to

Motown

Motown wasn't the name of a town or city—it was the name of a famous record label in Detroit, Michigan. It was named Motown because Detroit's nickname was "the Motor City," since cars were made there. The Motown sound combined soul music and pop music. Motown groups were almost all African American—Stevie Wonder, The Temptations, and Gladys Knight and the Pips. They were popular with everyone, though—black and white listeners alike.

make a record. Their dream was to go to Motown. More than anything, Michael and his brothers wanted to record their music for the Motown label.

No matter how many times Joe tried, he couldn't get Motown to pay attention to the Jackson 5. Finally, Joe decided that Motown would have to notice them if they won the biggest talent contest of all time—at the Apollo Theater in New York City.

The Apollo is a famous theater in Harlem, an African American neighborhood.

All the singers Michael loved had performed at the Apollo—people like James Brown and Stevie Wonder. A talent contest had been held there every Wednesday night for years.

So in the summer of 1967, when Michael was nine years old, Joe put all five of his boys into the family's VW bus and drove to New York City. Next stop, the Apollo!

Michael was dazzled by the huge, fancy theater. He

even loved the microphone—it rose right up out of the floor. Part of a tree trunk was near the stage. It was supposed to be good luck to rub the tree before going onstage. So of course that's what Michael and his brothers did.

But the Jackson 5 had something better than luck—they had talent.

They won the talent show.

Now would Motown call?

When they got home, Joe Jackson made a new rule. Phone calls could never last more than five minutes. Joe didn't want the line to be busy when Motown tried to reach them.

For months, they didn't hear from Motown. So Joe Jackson decided to accept an offer from a local record company called Steeltown. It was just a small studio in Gary, Indiana, but they recorded the first Jackson 5 song. It was called "Big Boy." Radio stations played it, and Joe sold lots of copies of it. But the Jackson 5 weren't going to get famous that way.

Finally, in July 1968, the call from Motown came. Michael and his brothers piled into their VW bus and drove to Detroit. They were going to sing for the head of the record company—Berry Gordy. If he liked them, they'd get a record deal!

As soon as Berry Gordy heard the Jacksons sing, he knew what a superstar Michael could be. He told them, "I'm going to make you kids the biggest thing in the world." He promised that their first record would be number one on the music charts.

Michael Jackson was only ten years old—but he was on his way to becoming a legend.

Chapter 2

Sunny California

In 1969, Berry Gordy moved his Motown offices to Los Angeles, California—and the Jackson 5 moved with him. Gordy wanted them to live in California so they could record music there. Joe and Katherine Jackson were still back in Indiana. They were closing up their house so they could move to LA, too.

For a while, Michael lived part-time with Berry Gordy. The rest of the time, he lived down the street with a neighbor. The neighbor was a famous singer named Diana Ross!

Diana Ross was the star of a Motown group called the Supremes. She taught Michael about art and music. She took him to museums and taught him to draw.

Michael loved Diana Ross. Living with her was one of the most special times in his life. He loved California, too. It was almost always sunny outside. He couldn't believe there were oranges on the trees. He and his brothers went to Disneyland.

Pretty soon, Berry Gordy brought the Jackson boys into his new recording studio. He had a song for them. It was called "I Want You Back."

Berry Gordy made the boys record it over and over again. For weeks! Michael listened to every word Berry Gordy said. Little by little, Michael was learning all about the music business—and he was learning from one of the best.

Berry Gordy turned the Jackson 5 into pop stars. He gave them new outfits and new hairstyles. He had someone teach the boys how to answer questions from reporters. They were tested on the answers! They were given lessons in table manners. Of course that was easy for Michael and his brothers. Their mother had insisted on good manners all their lives.

When "I Want You Back" came out in November 1969, it sold two million copies in six weeks! It was a number one hit, just as Berry Gordy had promised. Their next three singles were number one hits, too. The Jackson 5 were stars. And Michael Jackson was the most famous one in the group.

They did television shows with Diana Ross. They signed autographs. They went on the *Ed Sullivan Show*—a famous Sunday-night TV show. It was the same show where the Beatles had performed.

They played concerts in huge arenas like Madison Square Garden in New York. Mobs of fans—screaming girls—crowded around Michael wherever he went. Michael loved performing. He was never happier than when he was onstage. But he didn't like being crushed by fans. Sometimes girls scratched his face by accident. It was scary!

To avoid the crowds of fans, Michael and his brothers hid in their hotel rooms most of the time. They didn't have much freedom, but they did have a lot of fun together. They made fake phone calls. Then they giggled and hung up. They ordered room-service meals for other people's rooms. They held races in the hallways and had pillow fights. Michael loved to play pranks and practical jokes. His brothers did, too. Sometimes they dropped water balloons on people from the hotel windows!

Now the Jacksons were rich enough to buy their own fancy house in California. Joe and Katherine bought a house not far from Hollywood. The whole family lived there together for many years.

His early teen years were good times for Michael. He was still working nonstop, but at least he was having some fun in his time off.

But as Michael got older, he got hit with all the problems that teenagers face. Except he wasn't like other teenagers. He was a famous singer. It was a lot harder to grow up being Michael Jackson—rich, famous, and with everyone watching all the time.

Chapter 3

Big Changes

By the time Michael was fourteen years old, he was miserable about the way he looked. He wasn't a cute little kid anymore. Often fans were surprised or disappointed when they met him. Some didn't even recognize him! They were hoping to meet the person who was on the cover of the Jackson 5 albums. Now he was a skinny teenager, growing tall.

The growth spurt wasn't the worst part. The worst part was his face. It broke out in pimples. His father and brothers teased him about it all the time. They teased him about his nose, too, saying it was too big.

Michael couldn't stand to look in the mirror. He even

washed his face in the dark, so he wouldn't have to look at himself!

From then on, Michael became super shy. He spoke in a very soft voice. He couldn't look people in the eye. He didn't even want to go out in public.

Michael's father didn't show much respect for Michael's feelings. Sometimes he brought fans into Michael's hotel room—while Michael was sleeping! Michael would wake up, and his fans would be right there, staring at him.

As time went on, Michael focused more and more on looking better. For Michael that meant finding ways to cover up his face.

Other things were changing in Michael's life, too. As he got older, he wanted to have more control over his own music. He wanted to write his own songs.

Michael talked to Berry Gordy about it, but Gordy said no.

So in 1976, the Jacksons left Motown. Michael was

almost eighteen years old. Joe made a deal with CBS Records for $3.5 million. That was a huge amount of money. Best of all, now Michael could write his own songs and control how the records sounded.

The only problem was that Jermaine Jackson didn't want to leave Motown. He was an adult now—and he had married Berry Gordy's daughter. So Jermaine quit the band. Randy Jackson took Jermaine's place. From then on, they couldn't call themselves the Jackson 5. Motown owned the name. So they just called themselves The Jacksons.

Michael was sorry to leave Berry Gordy, but Michael was a smart businessman by now.

Two year later, Michael got an exciting call from Diana Ross. She wanted him to be in a movie with her. Diana was going to star in *The Wiz*. The story was based on *The Wizard of Oz*, but it was set in New York City. Michael would get to play the Scarecrow. He was so happy because he had to wear a lot of makeup. It covered up his pimples. He also loved dancing in the film.

Diana complained that Michael learned his dances too fast and it made everyone else look bad. Michael couldn't help it. When it came to dancing, he was just that good.

The Wiz was not a hit. In fact, it was a flop. But Michael had loved making the movie. That was part of his dream now— to become a movie star.

On the set of *The Wiz*, Michael became good friends with a man who would change his life in many ways. That man was Quincy Jones.

Quincy was a brilliant record producer, just like Berry Gordy. But Quincy didn't work for Motown. He worked for himself. Like Berry, he was kind and helpful to Michael. One day, on the movie set, Quincy heard Michael pronounce a word wrong. Very quietly, he told Michael how to say it the right way. Michael was so grateful. From that moment on, the two of them were friends. Quincy became like a father to Michael.

Fred Astaire (1899-1987)

Fred Astaire was one of the movie stars Michael Jackson loved. Astaire was also the most famous dancer in America. He was a tap dancer who moved almost like a ballet dancer. He made many movies with fantastic dances in them. In one movie, Fred Astaire danced right up the side of a wall—and then seemed to dance on the ceiling!

Michael studied Fred Astaire's dance moves. When he wrote a book about his own life, Michael put a note in the front. It said, "This book is dedicated to Fred Astaire."

The day after Michael first did the Moonwalk on TV, he got a phone call from Fred Astaire. Fred was calling to tell Michael he could really move!

The timing was perfect for Michael. Now that Michael had left Motown, he was getting ready to make some changes in his own music. Quincy Jones was the right person to help make that happen.

In August 1979, Michael put out a solo album produced by Quincy. The album was called *Off the Wall*. Quincy talked other big stars into writing songs for the album. Paul McCartney—one of the Beatles—wrote one of the songs.

That same month, Michael turned twenty-one. Now he was old enough to make all his own decisions.

His first decision was a big one. He decided to fire his manager. But his manager was his father! Michael knew that his father had done a pretty good job for their family at first. He had created the Jackson 5 and brought them to Motown.

But Michael didn't want Joe running his life anymore. From now on, Michael was going to run his own life—and no one would be able to tell him what to do.

Chapter 4

Fame and Fortune

Now that Joe wasn' t managing Michael' s career, Michael needed to hire someone smart to help him. The first person he hired was a lawyer named John Branca. Over the next several years, Branca helped Michael get the best deals a record company had ever offered a singer up to that time.

Michael's first solo album with CBS was a big success. Four songs from the album were in the top ten on the music charts. In 1980, Michael won a Grammy Award—the highest award in the music business.

But was he happy?

No. Michael was upset because he only won *one* Grammy.

Michael was angry because the award was for Best Male

R&B Vocal Performance. "R&B" stands for "rhythm and blues." Most R&B singers are African American. Michael felt the Grammys were saying, "That's a great album—for a black singer. But it's not good enough for the rest of pop music."

Michael was determined to win Record of the Year next time.

With Quincy as the producer, Michael went into the studio in 1982 and started recording new songs. He recorded four he had written himself. One song was a duet. Paul McCartney sang it with him. It was called "The Girl Is Mine."

The album, called *Thriller*, also had other huge hits on it. "Billie Jean" and "Beat It"— both written by Michael—each went straight to number one on the charts. So did the song "Thriller," which was written by someone else.

Before long, *Thriller* became the best-selling album of all time. It sold ten million copies the first year it came out, 1983. Over the years, it sold over one hundred million copies. No album has ever sold more copies than *Thriller*. In just four years, Michael earned more than $190 million.

What made *Thriller* such a huge success? Many things. First, Quincy and Michael worked so well together. They made musical magic happen. Second, Michael was at the peak of his powers as an entertainer. He had been in the music business for nineteen years. He was a pro. He knew he needed to take his time—just as Berry Gordy had taught him—recording the songs over and over until they were perfect.

Sometimes Michael stayed up all night memorizing lyrics. Then the next day, they turned the lights out in the studio and recorded in the dark. That put Michael in a private mood, so he could put all his emotions and feelings into the song.

Michael and Quincy spent many months recording the album. They remixed the music over and over again, to get the sound just right.

Another reason *Thriller* was such a huge hit was because of its music videos. Michael thought of them as mini movies. He put all his energy and talent into them. The first one was for "Billie Jean."

At first, though, Michael couldn't get his videos on television.

Why not?

MTV, the new music-video channel, had only been around for one year. MTV thought their viewers only wanted to see white performers.

The president of CBS Records called up MTV.

He gave them a warning. He said that MTV wouldn't be allowed to play music videos by famous white stars at CBS— like Bruce Springsteen and Billy Joel—unless they played Michael Jackson.

So MTV gave in. They played the "Billie Jean" video. That made all the difference. *Thriller* suddenly became a number one album on all the music charts—not just the "black music" charts!

Michael made two more incredible videos from *Thriller*. The first one was for the song "Beat It." It was a video about street gangs. Michael used real gang members from Los Angeles to act in it.

His best, biggest, and most expensive music video was for the song "Thriller" itself. Michael wanted it to look as if he were changing into a werewolf. He hired a director of horror movies. The video even had a dance scene with zombies.

When it was time for the Grammy Awards, Michael got twelve nominations for the *Thriller* album. He was so happy, he whooped and screamed and danced around the house.

On the night of the Grammy Awards, he won eight times! "Beat It" won Record of the Year. *Thriller* won Album of the Year.

Shortly after that, Michael was invited to the White

House to meet President Ronald Reagan. Would this be enough to make Michael Jackson happy? Was he finally satisfied with his success?

Did Michael Have Perfect Pitch?

Perfect pitch is the ability to name any musical note, just by hearing it.

Michael Jackson had not been trained to read music, so he couldn't name the notes. But he was just as in tune as someone with perfect pitch. Michael never hit a bad note—and it drove him crazy when other people did.

One time, Mick Jagger from the Rolling Stones sang with Michael and hit a bad note. Michael never wanted to sing with him again. He said Mick sang flat!

Quincy Jones's recording engineer said that Michael Jackson was one of the few people whose singing never had to be fixed in the studio. It was always perfect, just the way he sang it.

Chapter 5

Scarred and Burned

After *Thriller*, Michael Jackson was the most famous pop star in the world.

Still, there was a deep sadness in him. It was probably left over from his unhappy childhood. He felt lonely. It seemed as if no one could understand him.

To the outside world, Michael looked like the huge star he was. He wore fabulous clothes and costumes onstage. Fans everywhere tried to copy him. One of his most famous costumes was a military jacket. It was covered in gold braids, sparkly rhinestones, and jewels. His hair was long and wavy. He often wore sunglasses.

On the inside, though, he was still shy and didn't feel

good about his looks. Michael had a skin disorder and wore a lot of makeup to conceal it. He also used a skin-bleaching cream.

He had already had two nose jobs. Nose jobs are surgeries to make someone's nose smaller.

Then, in January 1984, Michael had a terrible accident. He was shooting an ad for Pepsi, in a big auditorium in LA. Crowds of fans were in the audience, watching. Michael was supposed to walk down some steps on the stage. Sparks and fireworks were going off beside him. All at once, his hair caught on fire!

At first, Michael didn't even realize what had happened. He kept dancing and spinning. Then his hands suddenly flew up to his head.

Michael was rushed to the hospital. He had very bad burns. He had to have surgery. His scalp would never really be the same. Afterward, the doctors gave him drugs for the pain.

Up till then, Michael Jackson had never used drugs. But he took the pain pills that his doctors gave him. Over time, he got addicted to those drugs and didn't want to stop.

Two good things came out of the Pepsi accident, though. Pepsi gave Michael $1.5 million to donate to the burn center at the hospital where he had been treated.

Pepsi also gave Michael a deal of just over $5.2 million to make more Pepsi ads. John Branca helped Michael make the deal. Michael was already famous and loved by millions. But now he was about to become one of the richest men in the music world.

Chapter 6

Buying the Beatles

Michael had been in the music business long enough to know how it worked. Often, the record companies got rich, while the singers and songwriters didn't. Why? A big part of the money came from owning the rights to the songs. Sure, the singers got paid for each record that they sold. But sometimes, they only got one penny per copy—or less! They couldn't get rich that way.

The Jackson 5 had never owned the rights to their own songs. For one thing, they hadn't written them. Besides, Berry Gordy made all his singers sign a contract saying that Motown owned the songs.

The Beatles had the same thing happen to them. They

wrote so many great songs—but they had given away the rights. The Beatles made a lot of money from their records and ticket sales to their concerts. They made money from movies and TV. Still, they didn't own their own songs— and that's where the big money was.

When Michael met Paul McCartney in 1981, Paul told him a secret. He was buying up the rights to other singers' big hits. Paul had a list of songs he had bought. He called it his catalog. He was getting rich from owning other people's music. Paul said Michael should do the same thing. So Michael asked his lawyer, John Branca, to keep an eye out for songs that Michael could buy.

One day in 1984, Branca said a new catalog of songs was for sale—the Beatles' songs! Michael couldn't believe it. He wanted that catalog, no matter how much he had to pay for it.

It was going to be tricky, though. What if Paul McCartney wanted to buy his own songs back?

John Branca asked Paul McCartney's lawyer whether Paul was planning to do that. The lawyer said no—it was too expensive. But Paul didn't realize that Michael Jackson wanted to buy the Beatles' songs. If he had known, he might have changed his mind.

Branca offered $30 million for the catalog. Other people bid higher. The price kept going up. Pretty soon, some of the smartest people in New York and Hollywood were telling Michael he was crazy. He was spending way too much money.

Michael didn't listen. It took a couple of months, but Branca finally won the bidding war. Michael Jackson bought the Beatles' songs for $47.5 million.

Buying the Beatles' songs turned out to be the smartest thing Michael ever did. Within ten years, the catalog was worth more than $150 million. It brought in payments of $10 million to Michael each year. Today, it's worth $1 billion!

Paul McCartney was upset about it, though. He called

Michael to talk. After all, they were friends.

Paul said that just like Michael and the Jackson 5, the Beatles had gotten a very bad deal when they were young. Now that Michael owned the songs, would he consider giving the Beatles a better share of the profits?

Michael said no. Even though Michael had a soft voice and shy personality, he was a hard businessman. And to him, this was just a business deal.

"We Are the World"

In 1985, Michael wrote a song with Lionel Richie called "We Are the World." The song was written for charity. Most of the money from the record sales would be used to help starving people in the African countries of Ethiopia and Sudan.

Quincy Jones produced the record. He got a group of famous singers to come into the studio all at once. Bob Dylan was there. So were Bruce Springsteen, Stevie Wonder, Tina Turner, Billy Joel, Cyndi Lauper, Ray Charles, Diana Ross, and many more. Of course Michael Jackson and Lionel Richie sang solos, too.

The record sold millions of copies and won three Grammy Awards. A video of the recording session was shown on MTV. It became a huge hit as well. More than $63 million were raised to buy food, clothing, and medicine.

Chapter 7

Wacko Jacko

Now that he was so rich, Michael could do almost anything he wanted. No one dared to tell him no—at least not his family or friends. Sometimes Branca did warn Michael not to do things. But even then, Michael just went ahead and followed his own heart.

A lot of the things Michael wanted to do seemed totally crazy.

In 1986, Michael visited a hospital and saw a glass box—like a clear coffin. It was called a hyperbaric chamber. It was for sick people who needed extra oxygen. Michael got inside the box and had his picture taken. Then he had the picture sent to newspapers. He said he slept in there every night, so he could live to be 150 years old.

The story wasn't true. Michael was just kidding around. He had read a book by P. T. Barnum, a famous circus owner. Barnum wrote that there was no such thing as bad publicity. Michael thought that was true.

Next, Michael created another weird story. He let people think that he wanted to buy the Elephant Man's bones. The Elephant Man, Joseph Merrick, was a real person who lived in England in the 1800s. He was part of a circus sideshow. The circus put him on display because his face and hands were very deformed.

When the newspapers heard about this, they thought Michael Jackson had lost his mind. One newspaper called him "Wacko Jacko." The nickname stuck.

In 1988, Michael got a pet chimp named Bubbles. He told people he slept with the chimp. He took Bubbles to dinner with him.

Michael was rich and famous. Yet he seemed no happier

than when he was younger. He still hated his looks. He kept having surgery on his face. Finally, he had so many that the tip of his nose was almost gone!

Michael had surgery to put a dimple in his chin. He started wearing a surgical mask over his face afterward to cover the scars until his chin healed. But some people thought Michael was just crazy and afraid of germs.

Michael looked very strange in some pictures. Newspapers kept calling him Wacko Jacko. It hurt his feelings. But he had tried to get attention in the wrong way. Now he regretted it—and wanted to get as far away from the public as he could.

In 1988, he found a good place to hide. He bought Neverland Valley Ranch in Santa Barbara County, California. It was nearly three thousand acres—much larger than most big city parks.

Neverland was like a dream come true for Michael. It was his private amusement park! It had a Ferris wheel, a small train, bumper cars, a pirate-ship ride, a roller coaster, a petting zoo, and much more. There were statues of children everywhere. Wild animals roamed around. A huge outdoor clock, as big as a building, was surrounded by the word *Neverland* spelled out in flowers. Of course there was a swimming pool, a movie theater, and a giant collection of video games. Michael also built a huge house for himself, and smaller guesthouses.

Michael had never had a real childhood—he had worked since he was five years old. At Neverland, he could play all day. It was perfect—except for one thing. Who could he enjoy it with?

Michael still loved his family, but he didn't want to live with them anymore. He felt his family asked him for things too often. They wanted him to tour with the The Jacksons again. Michael didn't want to do that.

So Michael moved into Neverland all by himself. It was a very private place, with a huge gate around it. Most of the time, Michael Jackson was very much alone.

Trouble

Michael had always loved spending time with children. Whenever he could, he found ways to be kind and generous to them. Sometimes he visited sick children in the hospital. Then he'd invite them and their families to come stay at Neverland. He bought bags of toys and spent hours putting batteries in them. He gave the toys to kids who came to see him backstage at his concerts.

As time went by, Michael became close friends with several young boys. Some people thought he was too close to some of them. Sometimes Michael took the boys on tour with him.

Over time, one boy's parents grew worried. The boy said Michael had touched him in a way grown-ups should not touch children. In 1993 the police got involved, and stories came out in the newspapers. Michael denied everything. He said that the parents just wanted money from him and were lying to get it. In the end, Michael paid the family millions of dollars so that they would drop their case against him.

Years later, another boy said Michael touched him in a way that was wrong. This time, Michael had to go to court. But many of Michael's young friends were on his side. They came to court to speak up for him. They said Michael had never done anything wrong to them. At the end of the trial, he was found not guilty and didn't go to jail. For the rest of his life, Michael insisted that he had never done anything wrong.

Chapter 8

A Family of His Own

Michael had never dated much. For a short time, he went out with Tatum O'Neal. She had been a child actress and was the daughter of a movie actor. Michael liked Tatum because she understood what it was like to be a child in show business.

A few years later, Michael went on dates with Brooke Shields. She too had been famous both as a child model and an actress. After that, he didn't have a girlfriend.

But when troubles came up in his life, he wanted someone who could help him and understand him. He was terribly lonely. He had lost touch with Diana Ross. He was taking drugs—prescription drugs, but he was taking too many of them. He needed help.

Michael called his friend Lisa Marie Presley. She was the daughter of Elvis Presley, the first rock superstar. Michael and Lisa Marie had been friends for years. Now they talked on the phone a lot while he was out of the country on tour. One day, on the phone, Michael asked Lisa if she would marry him. Lisa was married to someone else at the time. But she said yes. She would marry him after she got a divorce.

On May 26, 1994, Michael and Lisa Marie had a very secret wedding. It was in the Dominican Republic in the Caribbean. Michael didn't even tell his mother about the wedding. Lisa didn't tell her family, either.

When they came back to America, Lisa and Michael kept the wedding secret for months. Michael knew that when the secret got out, there would be lots of publicity—and he was right.

The marriage lasted less than two years. One possible reason it ended was that Michael wanted to have children.

The King and the King of Pop

Elvis Presley was the first rock 'n' roll superstar. Like Michael Jackson, he became famous for the way he moved onstage. He also made movies and wore flashy costumes in his act. In the 1950s, teenage girls loved him, and guys wanted to be like him. He was so famous, he became known as "The King."

Michael Jackson wanted a nickname like "The King." He wanted to be as famous as Elvis had been. In 1988, MTV asked Michael to appear on their Music-Video Awards show. He agreed, but only on one condition. From then on, MTV had to call him the "King of Pop" every time they mentioned his name. It worked—from then on, everyone called him by that royal nickname.

But Lisa already had children. They divorced in 1996. But they stayed friends for a long time after that.

Michael remained determined to have children. If Lisa wouldn't have his baby, Michael would find someone else who would. The person he chose was another friend, a nurse named Debbie Rowe. Michael had met her at his skin doctor's office. Michael and Debbie talked on the phone all the time. When Debbie agreed to have Michael's baby and give it to him, he was thrilled.

He gave her lots of money and bought her a million-dollar house. He was very grateful that she was willing to have children with him without being his wife.

Michael's mother had a different idea, though. When Katherine found out that Debbie was pregnant, she wanted Michael to marry Debbie. Michael had always loved and respected his mother. He knew she was very religious. He couldn't say no to her about this.

So on November 13, Michael and Debbie got married

in a hotel in Australia. Only about fifteen friends were there with them. Debbie and Michael both wore black.

On February 13, 1997, Debbie had a baby boy. Michael named him Prince Michael Jackson. People thought the name was too fancy. Did Michael think his son was royalty? No. The truth was that Michael's own grandfather and great-grandfather were both named Prince. It was a family name.

Michael took the baby home to Neverland alone—without Debbie. A staff of nannies and nurses took care of the baby. Debbie never lived with Michael. She didn't act like the baby's mother.

Then on April 3, 1998, Debbie had another baby with Michael. This one was a girl. They named her Paris. The baby's full name was Paris Katherine Michael Jackson.

Again, Michael raised the baby without Debbie. She only saw the children a few times. Finally, Debbie decided she didn't want to be married to Michael any longer. She and Michael divorced in 1999.

A few years later, Michael announced to the world that he had a third baby. This time, Debbie wasn't the mother. Michael wouldn't say who the mother was. The baby boy was born on February 21, 2002. Michael named him Prince Michael II. His nickname was "Blanket." After that, Michael's older son was known as Prince Michael I.

Now Michael had a family, just as he had wanted. Would his life be easier? Were happier times ahead?

Sadly, the answer was no.

Chapter 9

Too Little, Too Late

All through the late 1980s and early 1990s, Michael continued to record exciting music. His album *Bad* came out in 1987. It sold millions and millions of copies. One song on the album was called "Man in the Mirror." It became one of Michael's favorite songs, even though he hadn't written it. The song talked about trying to change the world by changing yourself first. Michael donated all the money he earned from that song to a camp for children with cancer.

Michael's next album, released four years later, was titled *Dangerous*. It included one of his most interesting songs—a song called "Black or White." The words said that it didn't matter whether people were black or white. The music video showed dozens of faces—people of all colors—morphing or blending into one another. Almost every top-forty radio station in America played the song the first day it came out.

Michael was still a huge star and a brilliant, creative performer. But his personal life remained troubled. He started using prescription drugs again.

By 2005, he hadn't recorded a big hit album in years. He hadn't gone on tour. Some of his managers thought he was afraid his show wouldn't be good enough. If his show wasn't fabulous, Michael thought he'd be disappointing his fans.

For several years, Michael and his children lived in countries overseas. They lived in Bahrain in the Middle East for a long time. Then they moved to Ireland. Finally they moved back to the United States, to Las Vegas, Nevada. The whole time, Michael kept spending like a superstar. Every year, he spent twice as much money as he earned!

By 2007, Michael was in terrible money trouble. He

had borrowed a lot so that he could keep up his expensive lifestyle. But he had to pay his debts soon, and that might mean losing everything— including the Beatles' songs and Neverland.

Michael had to start working again. He needed to do big concerts and record a big album. So he agreed to do a concert series called "This Is It." Fifty concerts would be held in London, starting in 2009.

In the weeks leading up to the first concert, Michael rehearsed nonstop. Sometimes he felt good and enjoyed it. He was still a great singer and dancer. The backup singers would often watch and applaud. But Michael was worried sick. He still wanted to be perfect. What if he couldn't deliver great shows for his fans? He couldn't sleep at night from all the worry.

Once again, he turned to drugs. To help him sleep, Michael hired a doctor named Conrad Murray. Doctors are only supposed to do what is good for a patient. But Dr.

Murray did not do that. He injected Michael with the kind of drugs that are used in hospitals for people having surgery. The drugs were very dangerous. They knocked Michael out for the night. That was what Michael wanted.

On June 25, 2009, Michael Jackson died from an overdose of those drugs. Dr. Murray was charged with killing him accidentally. For his crime, he went to jail for two years.

When the world heard that Michael Jackson had died, millions of fans everywhere were shocked and sad. A huge memorial service was held in Los Angeles. It was broadcast on TV. At the funeral, many famous people spoke, including Berry Gordy. Diana Ross sent a message to be read aloud. Michael's daughter, Paris, spoke, too. She talked about how much she loved her father and missed him. Superstar singers performed songs in memory of Michael. Each of Michael's brothers wore a single white glove with sequins on it, to honor their brother. They sat in the front row with the rest of the family, including Michael's parents.

As part of the service, Jermaine Jackson sang Michael's favorite song, "Smile." The lyrics probably said a lot about how Michael Jackson felt much of the time. They said: "Smile, though your heart is aching. Smile, even though it's breaking."

Now that Michael was gone, people wanted to remember the good things about Michael. His talent was so huge. It had been a gift to millions all over the world. His singing and dancing had brought so much happiness to others. Sadly, though, performing seems to have been the only way he found any happiness himself.

He was only fifty years old when he died, but he was already a legend. In fact, at the funeral, Berry Gordy said that "King of Pop" wasn't a big enough title for Michael. He said Michael Jackson had simply been the greatest entertainer who ever lived.

The Jacksons—Where Are They Now?

After Michael's death, the Jacksons performed concerts in tribute to Michael all over the world.

Jermaine Jackson had a very successful recording career of his own. He made solo albums and won a Grammy in 1980. He also recorded duets with the famous singer Whitney Houston.

Jackie, Tito, and Randy have all performed over the years as musicians on other people's albums.

Michael's younger sisters both had careers of their own. LaToya recorded albums and appeared on reality TV shows.

Janet Jackson is a huge star in her own right. She's sold millions of albums, performed at the Super Bowl, and appeared on TV and in movies.

Timeline of Michael Jackson's Life

1958	Michael Jackson is born in Gary, Indiana.
1967	Jackson 5 play the Apollo Theater in Harlem and win talent contest.
	First record deal with Steeltown Records.
1968	Jackson 5 sign a record deal with Motown Records.
1969	Michael and family move to California.
1970	Jackson 5 have three hit singles in one year.
1976	Jackson 5 leave Motown Records and sign a deal with CBS.
1978	Stars in *The Wiz* with Diana Ross.
1979	Solo album *Off the Wall* produced by Quincy Jones.
1983	Performs the Moonwalk on *Motown* 25 television special.
	Thriller is released and becomes best-selling album of all time.
1984	Wins eight Grammy Awards.
	Burned during filming of Pepsi commercial.
	Buys the Beatles' songs.
1985	Writes and records "We Are the World".
1988	Buys Neverland Ranch.
1994	Marries Lisa Marie Presley.
1996	Divorces Lisa Marie Presley and marries Debbie Rowe.
1997	First son born, named Prince Michael Jackson.
1998	Daughter born, named Paris Katherine Michael Jackson.
2002	Second son born, named Prince Michael II.
2005	Goes on trial and found not guilty.
2009	Dies at age fifty.

Timeline of the World

1957 — *West Side Story* premieres in New York.

1962 — John Glenn becomes the first American to orbit Earth.

1963 — Martin Luther King Jr. gives his "I Have a Dream" speech.

— President John F. Kennedy is assassinated.

1964 — Nelson Mandela is sentenced to life in prison in South Africa.

— The Beatles appear on *The Ed Sullivan Show* for the first time.

1967 — Thurgood Marshall becomes the first black Supreme Court justice.

1968 — Martin Luther King Jr. is assassinated.

1970 — The Beatles announce that the band will be breaking up.

1971 — The Twenty-Sixth Amendment to the US Constitution lowers the voting age to eighteen.

1974 — Richard Nixon becomes the first US president to resign.

1977 — Elvis Presley dies.

1979 — Margaret Thatcher is the first woman to become prime minister of the United Kingdom.

1981 — MTV debuts.

1982 — The first albums on compact discs (CDs) are released.

1986 — The *Oprah Winfrey Show* airs on national television.

1989 — The Berlin Wall, separating East and West Berlin, is torn down.

1994 — Nelson Mandela becomes president of South Africa.

2001 — Apple launches the iPod.

2009 — Barack Obama becomes the president of the United States.

Bibliography

Greenburg, Zack O'Malley. Michael Jackson, Inc.: The Rise, Fall, and Rebirth of a Billion-Dollar Empire. New York: Atria Books, 2014.

Jackson, Michael. Moonwalk. New York: Doubleday, 1988.

Taraborrelli, J. Randy. Michael Jackson: The Magic, The Madness, the Whole Story, 1958–2009. New York: Grand Central Publishing, 2009.

Whitfield, Bill, and Javon Beard, with Tanner Colby. Remember the Time: Protecting Michael Jackson in His Final Days. New York: Weinstein Books, 2014.